Let's Talk About
When a Parent Dies

Elizabeth Weitzman

First published in Great Britain by Heinemann Library,
Halley Court, Jordan Hill, Oxford OX2 8EJ,
a division of Reed Educational & Professional Publishing Ltd.

OXFORD FLORENCE PRAGUE MADRID ATHENS MELBOURNE AUCKLAND
KUALA LUMPUR SINGAPORE TOKYO IBADAN NAIROBI KAMPALA JOHANNESBURG
GABORONE PORTSMOUTH NH (USA) CHICAGO MEXICO CITY SAO PAOLO

Manufactured in the United States of America.

02 01 00 99 98
10 9 8 7 6 5 4 3 2 1
ISBN 0431 03599 7

British Library Cataloguing in Publication Data
Weitzman, Elizabeth
Let's talk about when a parent dies
1. Parents – Death – Juvenile literature 2. Bereavement in children – Juvenile literature
I. Title II. When a parent dies
155.9'37

Acknowledgements
The Publishers would like to thank the following for permission to reproduce photographs: Cover photo by Guillermina
DeFerrari; page 20 © Earl Kogler/International Stock; all other photos by Guillermina DeFerrari.
Our thanks to Mandy Ross in the preparation of this edition.
Every effort has been made to contact copyright holders of any material reproduced in this book.
Any omissions will be rectified in subsequent printings if notice is given to the Publisher.

Contents

Words in **bold letters like these** are explained in the Glossary on page 23.

Marisa

When Marisa was eight, the worst thing she could ever imagine happened. Her father died.

At first, she didn't believe it. 'No!' she yelled, and she pushed her mother away and ran up to her room. She thought it was a lie. Her father would never leave her. He loved her too much.

But Marisa's father really had died, even though he loved her with all his heart. It was the start of a very hard time for Marisa and her family.

◀ You can't **control** how you feel when a parent dies.

Grief

You will have lots of **confusing** feelings after your mum or dad dies. You may feel sad, and angry, and sometimes you may even feel nothing at all.

These feelings are normal. They are all part of **grief**, the deep sadness that comes when you lose someone you love very much. Feeling grief is called **mourning**.

It may be hard to believe that things will ever get better. They will. But it may take a long time.

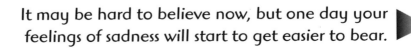

It may be hard to believe now, but one day your feelings of sadness will start to get easier to bear.

It's not your fault

Many children blame themselves after a parent dies. You may wish that you had tidied your room when your mum asked, or that you hadn't argued with your dad that last time. If only you had said that you loved him or her more often.

But nothing can ever make parents forget that their children love them. A parent's death is never a punishment. You are not to blame.

Nothing that you did or didn't do caused your mum or dad to die.

You can never love too much

Now that one of your parents is gone, you may think things would be easier if you hadn't loved them so much. You may decide to stop loving everyone, so that it won't hurt so much if someone else dies.

But this will just make everyone – especially you – feel much worse. Just now you need to give and get as much love as you can.

You may not feel like it, but in fact you need love more now than ever before. ▶

A common fear

Children who have lost one parent are often afraid that their other parent will die too. But it's very rare for children to lose both parents. In fact, it's so unusual that you should try not to worry about it.

But remember that no matter what, there will always be other family members and friends who will make sure that you and your brothers and sisters are loved and taken care of.

◀ **You will always have friends and relatives who love you and will take care of you.**

Changes

There may be changes in your life after your mother or father dies. You may not get any pocket money or new toys for a while, because your family needs to save money. Your other parent may have to work harder and get home later.

Try to help out around the house. If you do a few extra chores, it will make things easier for your family. It may even take your mind off your sadness for a little while.

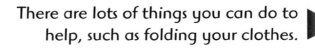
There are lots of things you can do to help, such as folding your clothes.

Talk about your feelings

You've never felt like this before. You may think that nobody else has either. You probably feel very alone. But many people have felt **grief** over the death of someone they love.

Talk to a family member or a friend about how you feel. Someone from your place of worship or a teacher will listen and understand too. Talking about your feelings will help you to feel better – and less alone.

Talking about your feelings with someone may help you feel better.

Acceptance

After a parent dies, it may seem as if he or she is still there with you. Every time the door opens, you may think it's him or her walking in as if nothing's happened. And then you remember the truth.

These feelings can be very painful, but they are normal. After a while they will start to fade. You will begin to **accept** that your mum or dad is really gone, and then things will get easier.

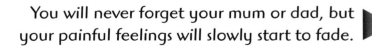

You will never forget your mum or dad, but your painful feelings will slowly start to fade.

The next step

Many months later – maybe even a year later – your **grief** will start to fade. When this happens, you'll be able to think of your mum or dad and smile. It's hard to imagine now, but you will want to have fun again.

When you feel ready, go and join your friends at the playground. Remember, your mum or dad would be happy to see you laughing again.

One day you'll be ready to smile and laugh again.

Memories

There are many different beliefs about what happens to people after they die.

But there's one thing you can be sure of – your parent will never completely leave you. As long as you have **memories**, your mum or dad will stay in your heart for the rest of your life.

Glossary

acceptance (ak-SEP-tans) – when you finally believe something is true

confuse (kon-FYOOZ) – to mix up

control (kon-TROLL) – have power over something

grief (greef) – the feelings of anger and sadness after someone has died

memories (MEM-or-reez) – things you remember about someone

mourning (MOR-ning) – feeling **grief** over someone's death

Index